Home Loans

To Roger,

Maybe this handbook will increase mortgage capabilities to equal golfing prowess.

Neil F.

Home Loans

Who, What, Where, When, and How?

By
Rick Ingersoll

AMERICAN HOME PRESS : Traverse City, Michigan

First printing 1991

Although the author and publisher have exhaustively
researched all sources to ensure the accuracy and
completeness of the information contained in this
book, we assume no responsibility for errors, inaccu-
racies, omissions or any inconsistency herein. Any
slights of people or organizations are unintentional.

Publisher's Cataloging in Publication Data
Ingersoll, Richard L., 1947-

      Home Loans
      1. Mortgage Loans

      HG5095   332.7   90-83994

ISBN 0-9626394-3-5

Printed in the United States of America

Dedication

To the children of this land of dreams I dedicate this effort. As you grow to appreciate this country you may well want to own a piece of it. The strengths this country were built on, hard work and honesty, will lead you to the American dream of homeownership.

To the *true* professionals (you know who you are) of the real estate and lending communities, I charge you with compassion and understanding in our clients' hour of need.

To the agents, originators, processors, closers and their support staff, go the "extra mile" and you will be "Dream Makers."

Foreword

For nearly all of us, buying a home is the largest investment we make in our lives. Unfortunately, we are required to make many mortgage decisions in very rapid succession, decisions we are generally not prepared to make.

Home Loans is a terrific guide to help all home buyers, whether it's your first, second, or third time around.

Today, there are many loans offered. Out there somewhere is a loan to meet your needs. By reading this book, you will be better prepared to ask the right questions and shop for, not only the right loan for you, but also the best lender. Look for one who meets your needs and is prepared to work for you and earn your business.

Take your time in reading this book and don't be afraid to ask questions as you shop for a lender.

Good luck in finding the mortgage loan for your needs and to help fulfill the American dream of home ownership.

Donald A. Maiolatesi
Executive Vice President
D&N Mortgage Corporation

Past President
Michigan Mortgage Bankers Association

Acknowledgments

Fifteen years in the real estate and mortgage lending industry have past so quickly. During those years several key individuals have influenced this project.

I would like to thank three people: Tom Edwards who gave me my first job as a lender. We've laughed and scratched our heads together as we've watched our industry change. Don Maiolatesi who gave me the courage and backing to start my own company. His often used phrase, "Rick, do the right thing," will always be with me. And Lee Hoyt, my mentor, a self-made man whom I look to daily for guidance and advice.

I would also like to thank the thousands of homebuyers I've met over the years. Your tears, fears, and anxiety have finally resulted in the joy and pride of obtaining the "American Dream." Let's hope all you've taught me will make the process easier for those who follow.

Contents

About The Author

Rick Ingersoll is a graduate of Western Michigan University and has received his G.R.I. designation through the University of Michigan and The Michigan Association of Realtors. He became a licensed real estate broker in 1978 and is also an approved underwriter for both the Federal National Mortgage Association and the Federal Housing Administration. Rick is also a state approved instructor for the licensing of realtors. At Northwestern Michigan College he has taught Credit and Collections and Real Estate Finance. Rick is co-owner of Midwest Mortgage, which he founded in 1984.

Rick speaks to local, state, and national groups. His down-to-earth style has been much appreciated by all those who come in contact with him. Contact Rick at:

Midwest Mortgage
333 East State Street
Traverse City, MI 49684

Introduction

"The time to buy is *now*" has never been more true. Over the last ten years, a smaller percentage of Americans have been able to buy their first home. The price of homes have been increasing faster than wages and the affordability gap continues to widen.

The problem is evident to us in the lending community. We are constantly developing new products to make housing more affordable. There are now hundreds of varieties of home loans, and more options than the potential home buyer can ever understand.

An informed buyer still has a chance of obtaining the American dream of homeownership. By understanding the basics and knowing what questions to ask, homeownership can still become a reality.

Home Loans

Chapter 1

So You Think You're Ready

Home Ownership is Truly the American Dream

1 So, You Think You're Ready

Tripped on the kids' skates again?
Did the landlord say the rent is going up?
Is it tax time and you haven't any deductions?
Was that same house for sale for $10,000 less last year?
Do you want a place to call your own?

One of those fits or you wouldn't be here. Home ownership is truly the American Dream. It offers stability, a sense of belonging, and, typically, it becomes your largest asset—the basis for your financial security. Later we'll discuss if you're able to afford a house. Let's first make sure you're ready mentally!

1. Do you like the community you live in? You will own part of your town and pay taxes for the services provided by the municipality. Are the schools highly rated? Is there adequate fire and police protection, or is the next community better organized and offer a higher quality of life?

2. Do you plan on staying for the next 3-5 years? It costs roughly 4% in closing costs to buy a home and 8% to sell it. If property increases 3-5% a year it will take 3 to 5 years to recoup your costs in and out of home ownership. If property is appreciating faster than 3-5%, your time frame can be shorter.

3. Do you feel secure with your present source of earnings? Lenders grant loans based on income that they deem to be "dependable and reoccurring." You know better than anybody; is your income secure?

4. Are your present living conditions unbearable? If you aren't happy where you are anyway, why not look at #5.

5. Can you own for the same monthly costs as you rent? In my hometown a nice 2 bedroom apartment costs $600 per month. You can borrow $50,000 and pay your taxes and insurance for $600 per month. Check it out in your town.

6. Is your personal life in order? One of the highest causes of home foreclosure is divorce. If this is a team effort are both members dedicated to the decision? As an unmarried individual remember, that future partners may have different opinions of home ownership.

WHEN - If you're satisfied with numbers 1-6 *now* is the time to buy. If prices are increasing in your area you probably can't save money as fast as they are increasing. An $80,000 home today at 5% inflation will be $84,000 next year and $88,200 the next. You can wait for interest rates to drop, but the increases in prices will offset your interest savings and you can always refinance when rates do fall. I've never met anyone that won by waiting.

Chapter 2

How Much Can I Afford?

The Three C's of Mortgage Lending

2 How Much Can I Afford?

Old rule of thumb - "Borrow twice what you earn in a year." Not a bad guideline! Current lending practices are a little more relaxed, so if you can live with the old rule you should be okay. For example, with a $30,000 annual income you can borrow $60,000; $40,000 annual income you can borrow $80,000.

The Three C's of Mortgage Lending

Lenders typically look at three basic factors to determine if your request should be approved

1. Credit
2. Collateral
3. Capacity

CREDIT

Your past credit history usually predicts how timely your future mortgage payments will be made. Slow payments in the past, judgments or bankruptcy may disqualify your loan request. If you have a legitimate reason for a past credit problem, be prepared to offer your lender a written explanation of the problem. A lender is more apt to overlook a past credit error if it was caused by lack of employment or medical reasons. Being late due to carelessness is not a good reflection. If possible, take a copy of a current "Consumer Disclosure Statement" available from your local credit bureau, to your prequalifying meeting and address any tardiness immediately. Hiding any past problems from your lender or neglecting to mention other current obligations is a serious mistake. At the time you apply for a loan you will grant your lender the right to investigate your past credit history. And, they are very thorough.

If you have limited borrowing experience, be prepared to offer your lender other evidence of your ability to meet your obligations. A letter from your past and current landlords may be helpful in addition to letters of reference from your doctor, dentist, insurance agent or utility company. They have all provided services prior to receiving payment from you and can be very helpful.

COLLATERAL

Lenders are interested in granting loans that are secured by marketable properties. Homes to be financed should conform to local zoning ordinances, be in good physical repair and be of fairly equal value with other homes in the immediate area. Plumbing, heating and mechanical systems should all be in working order and conform with current building codes. Lenders receive appraisals from professional appraisers who offer their opinion as to the properties' "fair market value." Even though the appraisal is just one individual's estimate of value, it is done after a thorough investigation of recent sales in the area of similar homes. Keep in mind that most loan programs have a maximum loan to value ratio and that the professional appraiser's estimate of the "fair market value" will help establish this ratio.

CAPACITY

This concerns your present earnings and your ability to meet your mortgage payments and other current obligations. Two formulas are typically applied to your earnings. In conventional loans, lenders will allow housing expenses of 25 to 28% of your gross monthly income. Housing expenses consist of principal and interest payments, real estate taxes, real estate insurance, association fees and special assessments. As an example, let us assume your gross monthly income equals $2,500 per month. A lender that allows 28% of your gross for housing expense would allow you to spend $700. By subtracting 1/12th of the annual real estate tax and insurance payments along with any association fees or special assessments, you will know how much you can afford for a principal and interest payment.

```
  $700.00
- 100.00  taxes
 - 20.00  insurance
 - 10.00  association fees
 - 10.00  special assessment
 _____
 $560.00  available for principal
          and interest
```

The second formula applied to your gross monthly earnings looks at your housing expenses and your other current obligations. Typically, conventional lenders will allow you to spend from 33 to 36% of your gross income for housing and other obligations. Other obligations may consist of auto loans or other installment loans, credit card debts, child support, alimony or child care expenses. Be prepared to offer your lender a complete list of your other obligations.

Two key things to remember when discussing your capacity are:

1. Lenders will only consider your earnings that are "dependable and reoccurring." If you receive sporadic overtime or bonuses, lenders may not include it in their formula unless it can be proven through history to be dependable and reoccurring. Other forms of income must also pass this same simple test.

2. If your other current obligations are relatively high, it can affect the amount you will be able to borrow for housing. As an example, if a lender uses 28% for housing expenses and 36% for housing and other

obligations, debts that total more than 8% of your gross monthly income will decrease the amount you have available for housing expenses. Lenders will apply both formulas to your income and allow the lesser of the two for your housing expenses.

Chapter 3

Calculating Your Borrowing Power

Principal and Interest Payments

3 Calculating Your Borrowing Power

Once you've determined what you can afford, refer to the chart to see what your borrowing power is.

CALCULATING PRINCIPAL & INTEREST PAYMENTS

Interest Rate	15 Years	20 Years	25 Years	30 Years
8.00	9.55	8.36	7.71	7.33
8.25	9.70	8.52	7.88	7.51
8.50	9.84	8.67	8.05	7.68
8.75	9.99	8.83	8.22	7.86
9.00	10.14	8.99	8.39	8.04
9.25	10.29	9.15	8.56	8.22
9.50	10.44	9.32	8.73	8.40
9.75	10.59	9.48	8.91	8.59
10.00	10.75	9.66	9.09	8.78
10.25	10.90	9.82	9.27	8.97
10.50	11.06	9.99	9.45	9.15
10.75	11.21	10.16	9.63	9.34

11.00	11.37	10.33	9.81	9.53
11.25	11.53	10.50	9.99	9.72
11.50	11.69	10.67	10.17	9.91
11.75	11.85	10.84	10.35	10.10
12.00	12.01	11.02	10.54	10.29
12.25	12.17	11.19	10.72	10.48
12.50	12.33	11.37	10.91	10.68
12.75	12.49	11.54	11.10	10.87
13.00	12.66	11.72	11.28	11.07
13.25	12.82	11.90	11.47	11.26
13.50	12.99	12.08	11.66	11.46
13.75	13.15	12.26	11.85	11.66
14.00	13.32	12.44	12.04	11.85

By multiplying the above factor by the number of thousand dollars requested you can determine your principal and interest payments.

Example: $50,000 at 10% interest for 30 years equals

50 times 8.78 = $439 per month principal and interest

It's that simple. There are only two ways to increase your borrowing power: 1) Increase your income, 2) Lower your debts

A word about the TERM of your loan. The options available are usually 10, 15, 20, 25 or 30 years. Lenders quite often will push for the longest term they can. Take the shortest term you can afford and save literally thousands. At 10% interest an extra $15 per month will take 5 years off the term on a $50,000 mortgage, $43 extra will reduce the term to 20 years, $98 extra will reduce the term to only 15 years.

If you feel uncomfortable obligating yourself to higher payments every month pay extra on your principal when you can afford it. The interest saving is tremendous.

Chapter 4

How Much Cash Will
I Need?

The 4th "C"

4 How Much Cash Will I Need?

"You mean I need more than a down payment?"

Sales Price
+ Closing Costs
+ Prepaid Item
- Mortgage Amount
= Cash To Close

The Fourth "C" - CASH TO CLOSE

This is sometimes the hardest thing for borrowers to obtain and understand. Lenders need to prove that you not only have the money for a down payment, but also have the funds to pay any closing costs, prepaid items and still have a cash reserve.

Let's assume you want to purchase an $80,000 home under a loan program that requires a minimum down payment of 5%. The down payment required would be $4,000.

The closing costs consist of all the paperwork charges for closing your mortgage loan. They may include origination fees, commitment fees, discount points, appraisals, credit reports, title work, surveys, recording fees and others. Every lender has different closing costs and it is best to discuss them with your local lender. Ask for, and make sure you receive in writing a "Good Faith Estimate of Closing Costs" and an Annual Percentage Rate Disclosure Statement." For this instance, let's assume the closing costs for our $76,000 mortgage are $3,000.

Prepaid items are items that lenders may ask to have paid in advance. They may consist of prepaid interest or interest from the day of closing until the last day of the month. Many lenders are writing mortgages with the monthly payments due on the first of each month and prepaid interest will apply. Your first year's homeowners insurance usually must be prepaid at the time of closing.

Many lenders require the escrowing of real estate taxes. This procedure calls for you to make monthly payments toward your future real estate tax bills, and lenders may require at closing a lump sum contribution toward the upcoming tax bill. For our example, let's assume the prepaid items total $1,200.

Our example so far shows we need $4,000 for a down payment plus $3,000 for closing costs and $1,200 for prepaid items. This $8,200 may not be sufficient to satisfy your lender. In many cases a cash reserve equal to 3 months' housing expenses is also required. If your house payment for principal interest, taxes and insurance equaled $800, the lender may want to verify that you have another $2,400 available for a total of $10,600.

Lenders will verify "cash to close" by sending verifications of deposits to your bank, credit union, stock broker, etc. Your loan request usually will not be approved unless you can verify at the time you apply that you have the funds available. Gifts from relatives may be used for part of your cash required to close, but it is wise to check with your lender to determine their individual policy on gifts.

Garbage Fees

Most closing costs serve a legitimate purpose.

Appraisals - determine "fair market value"
Credit Reports - determine your credit history
Surveys - show if the buildings are on the right property
Title Insurance - ensures the lenders interest in the loan
Recording Fees - properly notify the world of the lenders loan

But, "Garbage Fees" are nothing more than additional income for the lender or, you're paying for somebody else to do the lender's job.

Application Fees - Some lenders charge just to consider accepting your application for loan processing.

Underwriting Fees - Some lenders charge $100-$200 to make the decision to say yes or no to your request, in addition to your commitment fee, origination fee or points.

Tax Service Fees - Lenders hire separate companies to make sure your property taxes have been paid on time. Again, you pay the bill. If the lender collects money in your payment for taxes, shouldn't they know if your taxes have been paid?

Closing Fees - Many lenders have title companies handle the loan closing or disbursement of funds. It frees up the lender's time. Again, you pay the bill.

When you shop, look for "garbage fees." If two lenders are offering identical interest rates and points, the one with the least "garbage fees" will be cheaper in the long run. And these fees are not reflected in the calculation of "Annual Percentage Rate" which determines the true cost of borrowing.

On the following page is an example of a Good Faith Estimate form detailing closing costs.

(RESPA=Real Estate Settlement Procedure Act)

Estimated Settlement Charges

| APPLICANT(S) | John A. & Mary A. Borrower | | AMOUNT OF SALE | $80,000.00 |

| PROPERTY ADDRESS | 123 Main Street | | | |

☐ FHA ☐ VA ☒ CONVENTIONAL

| LOAN AMOUNT | $76,000.00 | INTEREST RATE | 10% |

This list gives an estimate of most of the charges you will have to pay at the settlement of your loan. The figures shown as estimates, are subject to change. The figures shown are computed based on sales price and proposed mortgage amount as stated on your loan application.

ESTIMATED SETTLEMENT CHARGES

NUMBERS FROM HUD-1 FORM	DESCRIPTION OF CHARGES	ESTIMATED AMOUNT OR RANGE From	To
801.	LOAN ORIGINATION FEE	$	to 760.00
802.	LOAN DISCOUNT	$	to 380.00
803.	APPRAISAL FEE	$	to 200.00
804.	CREDIT REPORT	$	to 50.00
805.	INSPECTION FEE	$	to
806.	MORTGAGE INSURANCE APPLICATION FEE	$	to
807.	ASSUMPTION FEE	$	to
808.	UNDERWRITING FEE	$	to 150.00
		$	to
		$	
901. (SEE BELOW)*	INTEREST ADJUSTMENT (Prepaid)	$ 20.82	to 624.65
902.	MORTGAGE INSURANCE PREMIUM	$	to 760.00
		$	to
1101.	SETTLEMENT OR CLOSING FEE	$	to 100.00
1105.	DOCUMENT PREPARATION FEE	$	to 60.00
1107.	ATTORNEY'S FEES	$	to
1108.	TITLE INSURANCE	$	to 315.00
1201.	RECORDING FEES	$	to 25.00
1202.	CITY/COUNTY TAX/STAMPS	$	to
1203.	STATE TAX/STAMPS	$	to
1301.	SURVEY	$	to 150.00
1302.	PEST INSPECTIONS	$	to 50.00
OTHERS:		$	to
Prepaid	1st. Year's Homeowners Insurance	$	to ??
Prepaid	Tax and Insurance Escrow Deposit	$	to ??
1400 & 103	ESTIMATED SETTLEMENT CHARGES		

TOTAL EST. CHARGES

(FROM ABOVE) * This interest calculation represents the greatest amount of interest you could be required to pay at settlement. The actual amount will be determined by which day of the month your settlement is conducted. To determine the amount you will have to pay, multiply the number of days remaining in the month in which you settle times $ 20.82 , which is the daily interest charge for your loan.

"THIS FORM DOES NOT COVER ALL ITEMS YOU WILL BE REQUIRED TO PAY IN CASH AT SETTLEMENT, FOR EXAMPLE, DEPOSIT IN ESCROW FOR REAL ESTATE TAXES AND INSURANCE. YOU MAY WISH TO INQUIRE AS TO THE AMOUNTS OF SUCH OTHER ITEMS." YOU MAY BE REQUIRED TO PAY OTHER ADDITIONAL AMOUNTS AT SETTLEMENT.

1. The Undersigned Acknowledges Receipt of This Good Faith Estimate of Charges.
2. The HUD Guide for Home Buyers, entitled, Settlement Costs.

APPLICANT _____   BY _____

APPLICANT _____   PER _____   DATE _____

Chapter 5

"Points"

Origination or Commitment Fees

5 "Points" The Mystery Solved

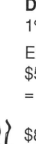

Definition - One point equals 1% of the loan amount.

Example:
$50,000 loan amount times 1% = $500 = 1 point

$80,000 loan amount times 1% = $800 = 1 point

Most lenders require points be paid. Lenders call them origination fees, commitment fees, or "points". Think of "points" as a bribe to get a lender to give you a certain interest rate. If a lender is offering his standard 30 year fixed rate loan at 10 1/2% with 1 1/2 points, you may be able to bribe the lender into 10 1/4% by paying 2 points. Or, if you are short of cash to close, the lender may offer you 11% with no points. When shopping for a loan you must look at the combination of "interest rate and points". Only you can determine if paying extra points for a lower rate of interest makes sense. As a general rule of thumb, if you don't plan on staying in your home for at least 5 years, paying extra "points" for a lower rate of interest is not a good idea. Check with each lender you see to determine what you'll save each month at a lower rate and divide the monthly savings into the cost of the extra "points" paid at closing.

Chapter 6

What Type is Best for Me?

Mortgage Products

6 What Type Is Best For Me?

FIXED, FHA, ARM, GPM, GEM, MGIC, VA, BI-WEEKLY, BALLOON, ETC...

The Products

The most popular mortgage product is the FULL TERM - FIXED RATE MORTGAGE. This mortgage calls for EQUAL MONTHLY INSTALLMENTS over a given term until the entire loan balance is paid in full. Each monthly payment consists of interest due on the outstanding balance - PLUS- a reduction of the principal. For example, a 30 year loan of $50,000 at 10% would have a monthly payment for principal and interest totaling $438.78. Of the first month's payment, $416.78 is interest due on the $50,000 balance and $22.00 is the reduction of the principal. In the second month, $416.48 is the interest due on the new balance of $49,978. The remainder of the payment, $22.30, is applied to the remaining principal balance. This process is repeated 360 times in a 30 year loan.

As you can see, each month as payments are made a greater portion of your payment is applied toward the principal because less interest is due on the constantly decreasing principal balance. The benefit of this type of loan is knowing every month exactly what your payment for the principal and interest will be. As your income increases year after year, the percentage of your monthly income needed to make your house payment decreases.

A twist offered by some lenders on the fixed rate mortgage is the BALLOON CLAUSE or CALL OPTION. This is definitely to the lender's advantage and should be approached with caution. The balloon gives the lender the opportunity to DEMAND the outstanding balance due at a time prior to the loan being paid in full. As an example, based again on a $50,000 loan balance at 10% interest over 30 years, BUT, with a 3-year balloon or call option, monthly payments would again be $438.78 BUT ONLY FOR 3 YEARS! At the end of the 3 years the lender could call the entire balance of $49,075.82 or the lender may renegotiate the interest rate with you. Lenders may initially offer lower rates on mortgages with balloons or calls, as they have the advantage of getting their money back in a shorter time period, or they can raise the interest rate after a relatively short period of time.

Adjustable Rate Mortgages

A relatively new product is the ADJUSTABLE RATE MORTGAGE. This mortgage allows lenders to adjust the interest rate on the out-standing balance at given intervals. With adjustable rate mortgages there are several key terms.

The INITIAL RATE is set by the lender and is typically lower than the rates offered on full term, fixed-rate mortgages. As an example, a $50,000 loan with an initial rate of 8% amortized over 30 years would have a monthly payment of $366.88, but as a one year adjustable rate mortgage that payment would only be sufficient for one year. The balance at the end of the first year would then be $49,582.31

and the lender could adjust your rate higher or lower and cause your payment needed to pay off that balance to increase or decrease over the next year.

The ADJUSTMENT PERIODS are typically every year, but other adjustment periods are available. It is important that you understand when the lender will be making adjustments to your interest rate and your monthly payments.

The adjustments in rate and payments are typically controlled by an INDEX and MARGIN. The INDEX is stated in your mortgage documents at the time of signing. This informs you as to what basis your interest rate will be adjusted.

One common index is the one year T-BILL (Treasury Bill) index which is published weekly by the U.S. Treasury. Another common index is the Federal Home Loan Bank Boards Cost of Funds Index. Prior to your adjustment date your lender will notify you of the index at that time. The lender will then add to that index the MARGIN or percentage over the index. Thus, the CURRENT INDEX PLUS THE MARGIN will determine your new interest rate.

Let me give you an example. Let's assume that at your adjustment date the current T-BILL index is 7.5%. Let's assume the margin is 2.5% over the index as stated in the mortgage document. This means that your new interest rate will be 10% over the next 12 months until the next adjustment date. Thus, the payment required to pay off your balance of $49,582.31 over the remaining 29 year term would increase to $437.55. In a one year adjustable mortgage this process takes place every year until the balance is paid in full. Therefore, you will not know from year to year what your payment will be. NEVER agree to an adjustable rate mortgage unless you fully understand the ADJUSTMENT PERIOD, INDEX and MARGIN.

As a protection for borrowers many adjustable rate mortgages offer ANNUAL and LIFETIME CAPS on increases in interest rates. A 2% annual cap indicates that no matter how high the index is at the adjustment date, your interest cannot be increased by more than 2% annually for any adjustment period. In our past example, if the T-BILL index had increased to 8.5% and the margin was 2.5% over the index, you would expect to pay 11% until the next adjustment date. But, the annual cap would prevent the lender from charging more than 10% or a 2% increase over the initial rate of 8%.

A LIFETIME CAP simply states that over the life of the loan the total adjustment up or down cannot be more than the lifetime cap. For example, an initial interest rate of 8% with a lifetime cap of 6% indicates that at no time can the interest rate be higher than 14%.

Make sure that your are protected from NEGATIVE AMORTIZATION. Negative amortization may allow your outstanding principal balance to increase if annual and lifetime caps protect you from dramatic increases in your monthly payments.

A CONVERSION or CONVERTIBLE ADJUSTABLE RATE MORTGAGE allows borrowers at specific times to convert their adjustable rate to a fixed rate mortgage for the remaining term. This clause is very popular with borrowers as it allows them to purchase homes with the lower rates available on adjustable rate mortgages and benefit from the security of knowing it is possible to switch to a fixed rate in the future.

When considering an ADJUSTABLE RATE MORTGAGE make sure the following terms are understood:

1. The adjustment period
2. The applicable index
3. The margin over the index
4. Are there annual and lifetime caps?
5. Is there the potential for negative amortization?
6. What is the highest monthly payment you could be obliged to pay over the life of the loan?
7. Can the adjustable be converted to a fixed rate? If so, at what cost? How will the fixed rate of interest be determined and when will you have the option to convert?

Graduated Payment Mortgages

GRADUATED PAYMENT MORTGAGES are offered in numerous forms. However, there are two major reasons for their existence. The first is to allow lower monthly payments in the first years of the mortgage, but with payments that increase as the years progress. These lower initial payments will allow one to qualify or be approved for a higher loan amount. The increase in payments are typically a percentage of your monthly payment. For example, a $500 per month payment may increase 7 1/2% per year for each of the first five years.

Then, the increases will level off for the remaining term. In this case, your payment structure would be as follows: year one - $500 per month; year two - $537.50; year three - $577.82; year four - $621.15 and, finally, $717.81 every year until the balance is paid in full.

Keep in mind that if the first year payment is not sufficient to cover the interest due on your loan balance at the present interest rate, you could face NEGATIVE AMORTIZATION. Again, negative amortization means that even though you are making regular monthly payments your loan balance is actually increasing. As the monthly payments continue to increase though, you will eventually catch up on the increasing loan balance, and finally, you will begin to pay down the principal balance until it is paid in full.

The second reason for graduated payments is for the faster equity build up by the borrower. For example, $50,000 at 10% for 30 years calls for a monthly payment of $438.78 for 30 years. But, let's suppose that each year your payment increases 7 1/2% and continues to increase until the balance is paid in full. This increased amount of your monthly payment is applied directly to the principal balance and will shorten the term of the mortgage considerably.

The philosophy behind the graduated payment mortgage is that as inflation continues so will your income, and if your income increases you can afford more each year for house payments. Take a good hard look at your past earning pattern and present advancement potential before agreeing to a graduated payment mortgage.

The Bi-Weekly Mortgage

A real newcomer to the mortgage market is the BI-WEEKLY MORTGAGE. This mortgage calls for payments every two weeks instead of once a month. Let me illustrate how it can save you money. A $50,000 mortgage at 11%

over 30 years calls for monthly payments of $476.17 per month. With a BI-WEEKLY mortgage, every two weeks you will pay 1/2 of the required monthly payment or, $238.09. Every two weeks you pay your outstanding interest and a principal reduction that is then deducted from your loan balance. With your next two week payment you are paying interest on that reduced principal balance. In addition, by making payments every two weeks you will make 26 payments per year or the equivalent of 13 monthly payments. This means that you will be paying $476.17 extra each year. But, by using this plan you will payoff your mortgage in approximately 20 years and save about $47,000 in interest expense.

Many lenders offering bi-weekly mortgages require you to maintain a checking account from which they can automatically deduct your payment every two weeks.

Construction Loans

Are specialized short term loans used by builders during the construction process to pay themselves, their suppliers, and their subcontractors. As the building progresses, typically every 30 days, the builder will draw against the construction loan to pay current material and labor costs. Interest is paid on the outstanding balance every month until the project is completed and the construction loan is paid off with the home loan proceeds. If you're considering building a new home, negotiate with your builder who will pay the closing costs and interest charges associated with the construction loan.

Basic Definitions

Before moving on to the various loan programs, let's cover some basic definitions.

LOAN TO VALUE RATIO is the amount of your loan request as a percentage of the property value. Property value is typically the lower of the property sale price or appraised value. An $80,000 loan request on a $100,000 sales price is an 80% loan to value ratio providing the appraisal supports the sales price of $100,000. If the sales price were $100,000 and the appraisal was only $90,000 most lenders would consider the loan value to be 88%. Many loan programs have maximum loan to value ratios.

MAXIMUM MORTGAGE simply indicates that a given loan program will allow a maximum loan of only so many dollars regardless of your ability to afford a higher loan amount and its corresponding monthly payments.

An ASSUMABLE MORTGAGE indicates that a future buyer of your home may take over your existing loan and its corresponding balance, payments, interest rate and other terms. Assumability is a very beneficial feature if your interest rate at the time you sell your home is substantially below the going interest rate. Be sure to check with your attorney to discuss any contingent liability in allowing someone to assume your mortgage.

Available Loan Programs

The VETERANS ADMINISTRATION PRO-GRAM offers eligible veterans the opportunity to purchase homes with little or no down payment. The VA does not typically lend to the veteran the dollars to purchase a home, but offers lenders protection from loss in the event the veteran does not make his or her monthly payments and the mortgage must be fore-closed. VA loans at present can be fixed rate or graduated payment mortgages with terms of up to 30 years. Because of the low down payment requirements and the opportunity to obtain a long term fixed rate mortgage, all veterans should investigate this program. A maximum mortgage amount with no down payment with VA does exist.

FHA or FEDERAL HOUSING ADMINISTRA-TION loans offer low down payments. Fixed rate, adjustable rate or graduated payment mortgages are available. FHA's variety of programs have different loan to value ratios and maximum mortgage amounts. As with VA loans, FHA does not usually lend the money to the borrower but offers the lender protection against loss in the event of foreclosure. THIS IS A GREAT PROGRAM FOR FIRST TIME HOMEBUYERS!

FmHA or the FARMERS HOME ADMINI-STRATION has been active in providing funds for housing in rural America. A division of the Department of Agriculture, their rural housing program offers fixed rate mortgages with little or no down payment for low to moderate income families for terms of up to 33 years. Applications can be obtained directly from the local Farmers Home Administration office.

Many states have STATE HOUSING AUTHORITY loan programs that offer below market rate loans through the sale of tax exempt housing bonds. As each state has a different program, it is suggested that you contact a local mortgage lender or your state housing authority for more details.

CONVENTIONAL loans are written by local lenders without the protection or funding of a governmental body. It is the local institution that provides the funds for your home purchase and they offer either fixed rate, adjustable rate, graduated payment or bi-weekly mortgages. Each lender will establish their own lending policy with regard to maximum mortgage, assumability and loan to value ratio. As the local lender makes the final decision to approve or reject your application, you will get your answer faster and with less paperwork if you apply for a conventional loan, but typically you will need a larger down payment than with a government loan.

Chapter 7

How Do I Shop and Compare?

Examining the Various Products

7 How Do I Shop And Compare?

Borrowing money for a home is similar in many ways to buying an automobile. With an auto purchase you would typically look at the various models offered by the different dealers in your area. With a home mortgage you will need to examine the various products to determine the best one for you and which program fits your ability to pay.

The three major sources of residential mortgage money are SAVINGS AND LOAN ASSOCIATIONS, BANKS, AND MORTGAGE COMPANIES. Other sources of mortgage money in your area may include CREDIT UNIONS AND REAL ESTATE FIRMS. An educated buyer is more apt to find the product and program they need. To begin, I would suggest contacting a savings and loan, a local bank and a mortgage company. Your local phone directory, real estate agent or referrals from friends and relatives can help you pick the most locally active.

Now that you know where to shop, WHO do you see? Whether from friends, relatives, a real estate agent or the receptionist at the lending institution, find out which loan officers are paid on *commission.* A commissioned loan officer has a vested interest in your success. They will appreciate the opportunity to discuss your financial position and in many cases will tell you how to improve your chances (e.g. save more cash, restructure your debt). In short, they are more apt to go the "extra mile" to help get your loan approved.

Chapter 8

Let's Go!

Qualifying from a Local Lender

8 Let's Go!

Now that you know what's on the market, if you are mentally ready, and where and who to ask for help, here's HOW to start.

Before looking at any homes, find out how much you can qualify for from a local lender. It's a waste of your time, the real estate agent's time and potentially a seller's time to have you making offers to buy homes you can't afford. Everybody involved in your home purchase will appreciate your preparedness. Contact at least three lenders (banks, savings & loan and mortgage company) by phone and ask for an appointment for a PREQUALIFYING MEETING. These lenders will always appreciate the opportunity to discuss your financial position without cost or obligation to you. Remember, lenders make money by lending money. They want to see you and want to give you a loan. If these three lenders can't discuss all of the following: conventional, FHA, VA, State Housing Authority Loans, keep contacting lenders until you've covered all these options.

BE PREPARED.

The following list of items will allow the lender to determine, according to their guidelines, how much you can borrow.

THINGS TO BRING
TO A PREQUALIFYING MEETING

Your last two years' W-2 forms.

Your most recent pay stub.

A list of *all* your current obligations including minimum payments required and outstanding balances.

A list of all your liquid assets including savings, checking, stocks, bonds and certificates of deposits.

If self employed, your last two years' federal income tax returns with all schedules and a current profit and loss statement on your business.

The prequalifying meeting gives the lender the opportunity to sell themselves and their services. You are shopping and the only way to shop is as an informed shopper. Ask questions.

Here's a list of **MUST QUESTIONS TO ASK.**

1. Which program will allow me to borrow the most based on my current financial position? (Probably Adjustable Rate Mortgage. Do you want the security of a fixed rate of interest?)

2. What changes in my financial position will allow you to lend me more money?

3. Do you service your loans locally?

4. Do you make the approval decision locally?

5. Based on the loan program you think is best for me, what is a *realistic* time frame from application to closing?

6. Based on my maximum allowable loan and the program you think is best for me, will you give me a written "Good Faith Estimate" of closing costs as per Real Estate Settlement Procedure Act guidelines?

7. Ask for the U. S. Department of Housing and Urban Development Settlement Costs booklet.

8. What is the "ANNUAL PERCENTAGE RATE" on the loan you are proposing? (If applying for an Adjustable Rate Mortgage ask for an ARM disclosure.)

9. Explain your procedure on when my interest may be "LOCKED IN" and what options are available to me.

10. How much cash will I need at time of application and is any refundable in the event you deny my loan request?

11. If I pay more "points" at closing, how will it affect my interest rate? (One point equals 1% of your mortgage amount.)

12. Why should I apply with you and your institution as opposed to the one down the street?

The following are a list of things to bring to the application and an example of a Residential Loan Application.

THINGS TO BRING
TO AN APPLICATION

Your purchase agreement with a complete address and legal description. IF YOU ARE BUILDING, A SET OF PLANS AND SPECIFICATIONS PROVIDED BY YOUR BUILDER. **YOUR LENDER, BY THE APPRAISAL, IS DETERMINING THE VALUE OF THE "COLLATERAL."**

Account numbers (with addresses and zip codes) for all savings, checking, money market, CD's and stock brokerage accounts. **YOUR LENDER WILL BE PROVING "CASH TO CLOSE."**

Account numbers (with addresses and zip codes) for all debts, including mortgages, credit cards, installment debts, child support payment and student loan payment. **YOUR LENDER IS VERIFYING YOUR "CREDIT."**

W-2's for the last two years and your most recent payroll stub. If you are self employed, your last two years federal tax returns with all schedules and a current year profit and loss statement. **YOUR LENDER IS VERIFYING "CAPACITY."**

Copies of any Land Contracts you are paying on, or receiving income from.

Rental Agreements or leases on any investments you have.

VA applicants should have DD214 or Certificate of Eligibility.

❶ Enter amount of loan you are requesting.

❷ Provide complete street address of property being purchased.

RESIDENTIAL LOAN APPLICATION

MORTGAGE APPLIED FOR	☐ Conventional ☐ FHA ☐ VA	Amount $ 50,000	Interest Rate %	No. of Months	Monthly Payment Principal & Interest $	Escrow/Impounds (to be collected monthly) ☐ Taxes ☐ Hazard Ins. ☐ Mtg. Ins.

Prepayment Option

Subject Property

Property Street Address 5127 Main Street	City Traverse City	County Grand Traverse	State MI	Zip 49684	No. Units 1

Legal Description (Attach description if necessary) Lot 12, Block 28, Traverse Pines Subdivision	Year Built 1978

Purpose of Loan: ☐ Purchase ☐ Construction-Permanent ☐ Construction ☐ Refinance ☐ Other (Explain)

Complete this line if Construction-Permanent or Construction Loan	Lot Value Data	Original Cost	Present Value (a)	Cost of Imps. (b)	Total (a + b)	ENTER TOTAL AS PURCHASE PRICE IN DETAILS OF PURCHASE
	Year Acquired	$	$	$	$	

Complete this line if a Refinance Loan		Purpose of Refinance	Describe Improvements ( ) made ( ) to be made
Year Acquired	Original Cost $	Amt. Existing Liens $	Cost: $

Title will be Held in What Name (s) John A. Doe and Mary M. Doe	Manner In Which Title Will Be Held Joint Tenants

Source of Down Payment and Settlement Charges
Savings and Sale of Present Home

❸ Be sure as to the source, cash or other assets that will be converted to cash must be verifiable.

❹ Indicate number of years at present employment. A minimum two year history is required. Also indicate if self employed.

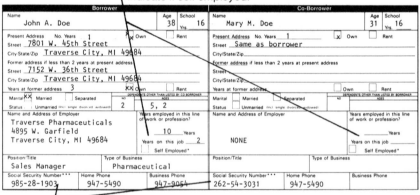

Borrower					Co-Borrower			
Name John A. Doe			Age 38	School Yrs. 16	Name Mary M. Doe		Age 31	School Yrs. 16

Present Address No. Years 1 ☐ Own ☐ Rent	Present Address No. Years 1 ☒ Own ☐ Rent
Street 7801 W. 45th Street	Street Same as borrower
City-State/Zip Traverse City, MI 49684	City-State/Zip

Former address if less than 2 years at present address	Former address if less than 2 years at present address
Street 7152 W. 36th Street	Street
City State/Zip Traverse City, MI 49684	City State/Zip

Years at former address 3 ☒☒ Own ☐ Rent	Years at former address ☐ Own ☐ Rent
Marital ☒☒ Married ☐ Separated	DEPENDENTS OTHER THAN LISTED BY CO BORROWER NO 2 AGES 5, 2	Marital ☐ Married ☐ Separated	DEPENDENTS OTHER THAN LISTED BY BORROWER NO AGES
Status ☐ Unmarried (incl. single, divorced, widowed)	Status ☐ Unmarried (incl. single, divorced, widowed)

Name and Address of Employer Traverse Pharmaceuticals 4895 W. Garfield Traverse City, MI 49684	Years employed in this line of work or profession? 10 Years Years on this job 2 ☐ Self Employed*	Name and Address of Employer NONE	Years employed in this line of work or profession? Years Years on this job ☐ Self Employed*

Position/Title Sales Manager	Type of Business Pharmaceutical	Position/Title	Type of Business

Social Security Number*** 985-28-1903	Home Phone 947-5490	Business Phone 947-9054	Social Security Number*** 262-54-3031	Home Phone 947-5490	Business Phone

❺ Required to assure accurate credit report information.

❻ List income of borrower and co-borrower separately. Enter all income on the correct line. All income must be verifiable.

Gross Monthly Income				Monthly Housing Expense			Details of Purchase
Item	Borrower	Co-Borrower	Total	Rent $	PRESENT	PROPOSED	Do Not Complete if Refinance
Base Empl. Income	$ 4025	$	$ 4025	First Mortgage (P&I)	180	$	a. Purchase Price $
Overtime				Other Financing (P&I)			b. Total Closing Costs (Est.)
Bonuses	208		208	Hazard Insurance	15		c. Prepaid Escrows (Est.)
Commissions				Real Estate Taxes	80		d. Total (a + b + c) $
Dividends/Interest	40		40	Mortgage Insurance			e. Amount This Mortgage ( )
Net Rental Income	48		48	Homeowner Assn. Dues			f. Other Financing ( )
Other† (BEFORE COMPLETING, SEE NOTICE UNDER DESCRIBE OTHER INCOME BELOW)				Other:			g. Other Equity ( )
				Total Monthly Pmt.	$ 275	$	h. Amount of Cash Deposit ( )
				Utilities	50		i. Closing Costs Paid by Seller ( )
Total	$ 4321	$	$ 4321	Total	$ 325	$	j. Cash Reqd. For Closing (Est.) $

❼ List monthly expenses on the appropriate line as they pertain to your present housing.

RESIDENTIAL LOAN APPLICATION

MORTGAGE APPLIED FOR ☞	Conventional ☐ FHA ☐ VA ☐	Amount ❶ $ 50,000	Interest Rate %	No. of Months	Monthly Payment Principal & Interest $	Escrow/Impounds (to be collected monthly) ☐ Taxes ☐ Hazard Ins. ☐ Mtg. Ins.
Prepayment Option						

Subject Property

Property Street Address 5127 Main Street ❷	City Traverse City	County Grand Traverse	State MI	Zip 49684	No. Units 1

Legal Description (Attach description if necessary) Lot 12, Block 28, Traverse Pines Subdivision	Year Built 1978

Purpose of Loan: Purchase ☐ Construction-Permanent ☐ Construction ☐ Refinance ☐ Other (Explain) ☐

Complete this line if Construction-Permanent or Construction Loan ☞	Lot Value Data	Original Cost	Present Value (a)	Cost of Imps. (b)	Total (a + b)	ENTER TOTAL AS PURCHASE PRICE IN DETAILS OF PURCHASE.
	Year Acquired $	$	$	$	$	❸

Complete this line if a Refinance Loan		Purpose of Refinance	Describe Improvements ( ) made ( ) to be made	
Year Acquired $	Original Cost $	Amt. Existing Liens $		Cost: $

Title will Be Held in What Name (s) John A. Doe and Mary M. Doe	Manner In Which Title Will Be Held Joint Tenants

Source of Down Payment and Settlement Charges
Savings and Sale of Present Home ❸

This application is designed to be completed by the borrower(s) with the lender's assistance. The Co-Borrower Section and all other Co-Borrower questions must be completed and the appropriate box(es) checked if ☐ another person will be jointly obligated with the Borrower on the loan, or ☐ the Borrower is relying on income from alimony, child support or separate maintenance or on the income or assets of another person as a basis for repayment of the loan, or ☐ the Borrower is married and resides, and the property is located, in a community property state.

Borrower	Co-Borrower

Name John A. Doe	Age 38	School Yrs. 16	Name Mary M. Doe	Age 31	School Yrs. 16

Present Address No. Years 1 ☒ Own ☐ Rent	Present Address No. Years 1 ☒ Own ☐ Rent
Street 7801 W. 45th Street	Street Same as borrower
City/State/Zip Traverse City, MI 49684	City/State/Zip
Former address if less than 2 years at present address	Former address if less than 2 years at present address
Street 7152 W. 36th Street	Street
City/State/Zip Traverse City, MI 49684	City/State/Zip
Years at former address 3 ☒☒ Own ☐ Rent	Years at former address ☐ Own ☐ Rent

Marital Status ☒☒ Married ☐ Separated ☐ Unmarried (incl. single, divorced, widowed)	DEPENDENTS OTHER THAN LISTED BY CO-BORROWER NO 2 AGES 5, 2	Marital Status ☐ Married ☐ Separated ☐ Unmarried (incl. single, divorced, widowed)	DEPENDENTS OTHER THAN LISTED BY BORROWER NO AGES

Name and Address of Employer Traverse Pharmaceuticals 4895 W. Garfield Traverse City, MI 49684	Years employed in this line of work or profession? ❹ 10 Years Years on this job 2 ☐ Self Employed*	Name and Address of Employer NONE	Years employed in this line of work or profession? ❹ ___ Years Years on this job ___ ☐ Self Employed*

Position/Title Sales Manager	Type of Business Pharmaceutical	Position/Title	Type of Business

Social Security Number*** 985-28-1903 ❺	Home Phone 947-5490	Business Phone 947-9054	Social Security Number*** 262-54-3031 ❺	Home Phone 947-5490	Business Phone

Gross Monthly Income				Monthly Housing Expense			Details of Purchase	
Item	Borrower	Co-Borrower	Total		PRESENT	PROPOSED	Do Not Complete If Refinance	
Base Empl. Income	$ 4025	$	$ 4025	Rent	$		a. Purchase Price	$
Overtime				First Mortgage (P&I)	180	$	b. Total Closing Costs (Est.)	
Bonuses	208		208	Other Financing (P&I)			c. Prepaid Escrows (Est.)	
Commissions				Hazard Insurance	15		d. Total (a + b + c)	$
Dividends/Interest	40		40	Real Estate Taxes	80		e. Amount This Mortgage	( )
Net Rental Income	48		48	Mortgage Insurance			f. Other Financing	( )
Other 1 (BEFORE COMPLETING, SEE NOTICE UNDER DESCRIBE OTHER INCOME BELOW.)		❻		Homeowner Assn. Dues	❼		g. Other Equity	( )
				Other:			h. Amount of Cash Deposit	( )
				Total Monthly Pmt.	$ 275	$	i. Closing Costs Paid by Seller	( )
				Utilities	50		j. Cash Reqd. for Closing (Est.)	$
Total	$ 4321	$	$ 4321	Total	$ 325	$		

Describe Other Income

▽ B—Borrower C—Co-Borrower	NOTICE: † Alimony, child support, or separate maintenance income need not be revealed if the Borrower or Co-Borrower does not choose to have it considered as a basis for repaying this loan.	Monthly Amount
		$

If Employed In Current Position For Less Than Two Years Complete the Following

B/C	Previous Employer/School	City/State	Type of Business	Position/Title	Dates From/To	Monthly Income
B	Northern Drug Services, Traverse City, MI - Pharmaceutical Sales Rep.				5/73 to 3/82	$ 3100

These Questions Apply To Both Borrower and Co-Borrower

If a "yes" answer is given to a question in this column, please explain on an attached sheet.	Borrower Yes or No	Co-Borrower Yes or No		Borrower Yes or No	Co-Borrower Yes or No
			Are you a U.S. citizen?	yes	yes
Are there any outstanding judgments against you?	no	no	If "no," are you a resident alien?		
Have you been declared bankrupt within the past 7 years?	no	no	If "no," are you a non-resident alien?		
Have you had property foreclosed upon or given title or deed in lieu thereof in the last 7 years?	no	no	Explain Other Financing or Other Equity (if any).		
Are you a party to a law suit?	no	no			
Are you obligated to pay alimony, child support, or separate maintenance?	no	no			
Is any part of the down payment borrowed?					
Are you a co-maker or endorser on a note?	no	no			

*FHLMC/FNMA require business credit report, signed Federal Income Tax returns for last two years; and, if available, audited Profit and Loss Statement plus balance sheet for same period.
**All Present Monthly Housing Expenses of Borrower and Co-Borrower should be listed on a combined basis.
***SSN optional for FHLMC
Freddie Mac Form 65 Rev. 10/86

Fannie Mae Form 1003 Rev. 10/86

This Statement and any applicable supporting schedules may be completed jointly by both married and unmarried co-borrowers if their assets and liabilities are sufficiently joined so that the Statement can be meaningfully and fairly presented on a combined basis; otherwise separate Statements and Schedules are required (FHLMC 65A/FNMA 1003A). If the co-borrower section was completed about a spouse, this statement and supporting schedules must be completed about that spouse also.

☐ Completed Jointly ☐ Not Completed Jointly

Assets		Liabilities and Pledged Assets			
		Indicate by (*) those liabilities or pledged assets which will be satisfied upon sale of real estate owned or upon refinancing of subject property.			

Description	Cash or Market Value	Creditors' Name, Address and Account Number	Acct. Name If Not Borrower's	Mo. Pmt. and Mos. Left to Pay	Unpaid Balance
Cash Deposit Toward Purchase Held By Ace Real Estate	$ 1,000	Installment Debts (Include "revolving" charge accounts) Co. Visa #008-1-91 Acct. No.		$ Pmt./Mos.	
Checking and Savings Accounts (Show Names of Institutions (Accounts Numbers) Bank, S & L or Credit Union) ABC Bank, Traverse ⑧		Addr. P.O. Box 9756 City Traverse City, MI 49684 ⑨ Acct. No.		30 / 15	450.00
Addr. 1010 Book Lane City Traverse City, MI Acct. No. 01-021234	12,500	Co. Acct. No. Addr. City		/	
Bank, S & L or Credit Union TCP Credit Union Addr. 123 Smart Street City Traverse City, MI Acct. No. 801-201	8,000	Co. Acct. No. Addr. City		/	
Bank, S & L or Credit Union Addr. City Acct. No.		Co. Acct. No. Addr. City Other Debts including Stock Pledges		/	
Stocks and Bonds (No. Description) 250 T.C. PH. @ $26.50	6,625	Real Estate Loans Acct. No. Co. T.C. Savings & Loan #00-00-1121 Addr.			34,000.00
Series EE Savings ⑩ Bond	1,000	City			
Life Insurance Net Cash Value Face Amount $ 50,000	750	Co. Western MI Bank #813-214758 Acct. No. Addr. City			18,000.00
Subtotal Liquid Assets	30,675				
Real Estate Owned (Enter Market Value from Schedule of Real Estate Owned)	82,000	Automobile Loans Acct. No. Co. TCP Credit Union #219806			
Vested Interest in Retirement Fund	2,900	Addr. 28 Front St.			
Net worth of Business Owned (ATTACH FINANCIAL STATEMENT)		City Traverse City, MI		100 / 22	2,200.00
		Co. Acct. No. Addr.			
Automobiles Owned (Make and Year) 1982 Oldsmobile	4,000				
1979 Ford	1,500	City		/	
Furniture and Personal Property	11,000	Alimony/Child Support/Separate Maintenance Payments Owed to		/	
Other Assets (Itemize) 28' Sailboat	24,000	Total Monthly Payments		130.00	
Jewelry	9,000				
Total Assets	$ 65,075	Net Worth (A minus B) $ 110,425		Total Liabilities	B $ 54,650.00

SCHEDULE OF REAL ESTATE OWNED (If Additional Properties Owned Attach Separate Schedule)

⑪ Address of Property (Indicate S if Sold, PS if Pending Sale or R if Rental being held for income)	Type of Property	Present Market Value	Amount of Mortgages & Liens	Gross Rental Income	Mortgage Payments	Taxes, Ins. Maintenance and Misc.	Net Rental Income
7801 W. 45th St., T.C. PS	RES	$ 50,000	$ 34,000	$ 00	$ 182	$ 95	$ 00
7152 W. 36th St., T.C. R	RES	32,000	18,000	277	180	47	48
TOTALS ▶		$ 82,000	$ 52,000	$ 277	$ 362	$ 142	$ 48

List Previous Credit References

▽ B—Borrower C—Co-Borrower	Creditor's Name and Address	Account Number	Purpose	Highest Balance	Date Paid
B/C	Bank of America, 1268 42nd L.A.	k-8224-1	Boat	$ 7,000	10/72
B/C	Morgan Dept. 469 12th Detroit ⑫	926-16488	Misc	800	11/80
B/C	ABC Bank Front St., T.C. MI	m-13-2864	Auto	4,8-0	9/82

List any additional names under which credit has previously been received _____

AGREEMENT: The undersigned applies for the loan indicated in this application to be secured by a first mortgage or deed of trust on the property described herein, and represents that the property will not be used for ⑬ illegal or restricted purpose, and that all statements made in this application are true and are made for the purpose of obtaining the loan. Verification may be obtained from any source named in the application. The original or a copy of this application will be retained by the lender, even if the loan is not granted. The undersigned ☒ intend or ☐ do not intend to occupy the property as their primary residence.
I/We fully understand that it is a federal crime punishable by fine or imprisonment, or both, to knowingly make any false statements concerning any of the above facts as applicable under the provisions of Title 18, United States Code, Section 1014.

_____ ⑭ Date _____   _____ ⑭ Date _____
Borrower's Signature   Co-Borrower's Signature

Information for Government Monitoring Purposes

The following information is requested by the Federal Government for certain types of loans related to a dwelling, in order to monitor the lender's compliance with equal credit opportunity and fair housing laws. You are not required to furnish this information, but are encouraged to do so. The law provides that a lender may neither discriminate on the basis of this information, nor on whether you choose to furnish it. However, if you choose not to furnish it, under Federal regulations this lender is required to note race and sex on the basis of visual observation or surname. If you do not wish to furnish the above information, please check the box below. (Lender must review the above material to assure that the disclosures satisfy all requirements to which the Lender is subject under applicable state law for the particular type of loan applied for.)

Borrower: ☐ I do not wish to furnish this information   Co-Borrower: ☐ I do not wish to furnish this information

Race/National Origin:
☐ American Indian, Alaskan Native ☐ Asian, Pacific Islander
☐ Black ☐ Hispanic ☐ White
☐ Other (specify): _____
Sex: ☐ Female ☐ Male

Race/National Origin:
☐ American Indian, Alaskan Native ☐ Asian, Pacific Islander
☐ Black ☐ Hispanic ☐ White
☐ Other (specify): _____
Sex: ☐ Female ☐ Male

To Be Completed by Interviewer

This application was taken by:
☐ face to face interview
☐ by mail
☐ by telephone

Interviewer _____
Interviewer's Phone Number _____

Name of Interviewer's Employer _____
Address of Interviewer's Employer _____

⑧ Provide name of institution, complete address, account numbers, and balances. (Use addendum when necessary)

⑨ Provide name of creditors, complete addresses, account numbers, monthly payments and balances. (Use addendum when necessary)

Assets			Liabilities and Pledged Assets			
Indicate by (*) those liabilities or pledged assets which will be satisfied upon sale of real estate owned or upon refinancing of subject property.						
Description	Cash or Market Value		Creditors' Name, Address and Account Number	Acct. Name If Not Borrower's	Mo. Pmt. and Mos. Left to Pay	Unpaid Balance
Cash Deposit Toward Purchase Held By Ace Real Estate	$ 1,000		Installment Debts (Include "revolving" charge accounts) Co. Visa #008-1-91 Acct. No.		$ Pmt./Mos.	
Checking and Savings Accounts (Show Names of Institutions (Accounts Numbers) Bank, S & L or Credit Union) ABC Bank, Traverse			Addr. P.O. Box 9756 City Traverse City, MI 49684		30 / 15	450.00
Addr. 1010 Book Lane			Addr.			
City Traverse City, MI			City		/	
Acct. No. 01-021234	12,500		Co. Acct. No.			
Bank, S & L or Credit Union TCP Credit Union			Addr. City		/	
Addr. 123 Smart Street			Co. Acct. No.			
City Traverse City, MI			Addr.			
Acct. No. 801-201	8,000		City		/	
Bank, S & L or Credit Union			Co. Acct. No.			
			Addr.			
Addr.			City		/	
City			Other Debts including Stock Pledges			
Acct. No						
Stocks and Bonds (No. Description)					/	
250 T.C. PH. @ $26.50	6,625		Real Estate Loans Acct. No. Co. T.C. Savings & Loan #00-00-1121	✕		34,000.00
Series EE Savings Bond	1,000		Addr. City			
Life Insurance Net Cash Value Face Amount $ 50,000	750		Co. Western MI Bank #813-214758 Acct. No. Addr.	✕		18,000.00
Subtotal Liquid Assets	30,675		City			

(left side vertical label: Statement of Assets and Liabilities)

⑩ Provide itemized list with description, number of shares and market value. (Use addendum when necessary)

⑪ List all property owned by borrower and/or co-borrower. Use monthly figures when listing income and payments. Income from rental property must be verifiable.

SCHEDULE OF REAL ESTATE OWNED (If Additional Properties Owned Attach Separate Schedule)

Address of Property (Indicate S if Sold, PS if Pending Sale or R if Rental being held for income)		Type of Property	Present Market Value	Amount of Mortgages & Liens	Gross Rental Income	Mortgage Payments	Taxes, Ins. Maintenance and Misc.	Net Rental Income
7801 W. 45th St., T.C.	PS	RES	$ 50,000	$ 34,000	$ 00	$ 182	$ 95	$ 00
7152 W. 36th St., T.C.	R	RES	32,000	18,000	277	180	47	48
		TOTALS ▶	$ 82,000	$ 52,000	$ 277	$ 362	$142	$ 48

⑫ List any company, bank or savings and loan with whom you have had credit history. Be sure to provide mailing addresses and account numbers.

⑬ Be sure to indicate whether you do or do not intend to occupy this property as your primary residence.

List Previous Credit References

B – Borrower C – Co-Borrower	Creditor's Name and Address	Account Number	Purpose	Highest Balance	Date Paid
B/C	Bank of America 1268 42nd L.A.	k-8224-1	Boat	$ 7,000	10/72
B/C	Morgan Dept. 468 12th Detroit	926-16488	Misc	800	11/80
B/C	ABC Bank Front St., T.C. MI	m-13-2864	Auto	4,8-0	9/82

List any additional names under which credit has previously been received _____

AGREEMENT: The undersigned applies for the loan indicated in this application to be secured by a first mortgage or deed of trust on the property described herein, and represents that the property will not be used for any illegal or restricted purpose, and that all statements made in this application are true and are made for the purpose of obtaining the loan. Verification may be obtained from any source named in the application. The original or a copy of this application will be retained by the lender, even if the loan is not granted. The undersigned [X] intend or [ ] do not intend to occupy the property as their primary residence.
I/We fully understand that it is a federal crime punishable by fine or imprisonment, or both, to knowingly make any false statements concerning any of the above facts as applicable under the provisions of Title 18, United States Code, Section 1014.

_____ Date _____   _____ Date _____
Borrower's Signature   Co-Borrower's Signature

⑭ Signature of borrower and/or co-borrower is required here as well as the date executed.

Chapter 9

Other Options

Suppose the Lender said "No!"

9 Other Options

Suppose The Lender Said "NO!"

All is not lost. You may not be destined to a life full of rent receipts. Consider these choices:

Lease with Option to Buy

If you have the income to qualify and good credit but not enough cash to close, many motivated sellers will allow you to lease the house of your dreams until you raise the necessary cash. In some cases part of your lease payments will be credited against the purchase price by the seller. Negotiate the price at the time of signing the lease, the term of your option and any credit against the purchase price. Remember the option to buy is your option, not the sellers.

Co-Mortgagor or Co-Signer

If your income is too low or debts too high, many lenders will allow another party (typically a family member) to co-sign or co-mortgage with you. A co-signer agrees to make the payments if you can't but has no legal interest in the property. A co-mortgagor owns the property with you and is also responsible for the payments. Using a co-signer or co-mortgagor should only be done with someone you trust. Many lenders will relieve your *Co* of their financial responsibility when you are able to qualify at a later date on your own.

Simple Mortgage Assumption

Many older loans (primarily FHA and VA loans) allow for the transfer of ownership without the new buyer (you) having to qualify for the loan. If a seller has a home for sale at $70,000 and a mortgage balance on an assumable mortgage of $60,000 all you need is to give the seller his or her $10,000 of equity and take over the payments. You will assume all the terms of the original loan including the interest rate, monthly payment and remaining term. With a *simple* assumption the original lender cannot say no. A *formal* assumption requires the lenders approval of your income, credit and cash to close. Know the difference and ask your real estate agent about homes with simple assumptions available.

Seller Financing

In many states and in many cases, sellers can act as your lender. Give the seller a down payment and make monthly payments of principal and interest to the seller. The terms and conditions of seller financing are strictly between you and the seller. A word of caution: Many sellers will help you finance the purchase but for only a short period of time. The contract between you and the seller may have a balloon clause. Make sure when the balloon comes due, you have the means to pay it off.

Order Form

Please send me _____ copy(ies) of **Home Loans** at
$9.95 each. $9.95 x _____ books = _____
(Michigan Residents add 4% sales tax)

Shipping instructions:
I'm adding $2.00 for the first copy and 50¢ for each addi-
tional copy _____ (Allow three weeks for delivery.)

Please rush the book to me. Instead of $2.00, I'm sending
$4.00 per book for First Class Priority Mail _____

Total amount of check is _____
(Please make check payable to Authors' Cooperative Publishing Services)

Name   _____

Address _____

       _____

Send a copy of **Home Loans** as a gift from me to:

       _____

       _____

       _____

AUTHORS' COOPERATIVE
PUBLISHING SERVICES

121 East Front Street, Suite 203
Traverse City, MI 49684
1 800 345-0096